Dead Dad Club

Julian Shendelman

Nomadic Press
2017

This book was made possible by a loving community of family and friends, old and new.

For author questions or to book a reading at your school, bookstore, or alternative establishment, please send an email to info@nomadicpress.org.

Published by Nomadic Press, 2926 Foothill Boulevard, Oakland, California, 94601
www.nomadicpress.org

First Edition
First Printing

Printed in the United States

Library of Congress Cataloging-in-Publication Data

Shendelman, Julian, 1988 –
Dead Dad Club/written by Julian Shendelman; illustrated by Arthur Johnstone
p. cm.
Summary: With a close eye on the past and an outstretched hand to the future, *Dead Dad Club* traces the death of a father and ties it to the rebirth of a son. Weaving together the hilarious and the grotesque, *Dead Dad Club* is a starkly honest collection of poems and musings that manage to make light of even the heaviest topics.
[1. POETRY / Subjects & Themes / Family; 2. POETRY / Subjects & Themes / Trans; 3. POETRY / American / General.] I. Title.

2017937393

ISBN: 978-0-9981348-5-7

The illustrations in this book were created using pen and marker on Canson paper.
The type was set in Garamond Premier Pro.
Printed and bound in the United States
Typesetting and book design by J. K. Fowler
Edited by J. K. Fowler

to my fellow members of the
Dead Dad Club: welcome.

CONTENTS

a ghost story is never about a ghost
because a body is not a house or a painting of the sky.
a ghost is not a story but the heat rising off an empty palm
or a closet stuffed with brittle newsprint, bent and yellow,
or a coat made of skin and silver hair, teeming with moths.
a ghost story smells like cedar because it used to be a tree:
and apparition of a recollection of a dream of an absence.

PROLOGUE

i can't believe they're allowed to cut people open
in an office building

a thin white woman with large breasts and a small son
her nose, carved from crumbling rock
skin, weak and tight, wrists, cigars in gold jewelry
fat glossy lips over a kitten sweater says
"leisure world"—where my grandparents lived until they didn't
an old man alone with his clipboard, looks fine
this is not a place for the sick
but a tailor's lobby
here for alterations, hemming
eyes roll over blocks of black text
i sign my life away, just in case, my credit, just in case

i take a green hospital gown and close the heavy door
wall of grey lockers, toilet, bank of floor-to-ceiling windows
i tower naked above the earth, grasping at my chest
the soft-and-thinning skin, the low, pink nipples
the pale stretch marks from a middle school growth spurt
the new crop of dark hair from the center of my sternum
the weight of it all, balancing in my palms like a sacrificial lamb
or a teeming bowl of warm water

my father's muscular calves in white compression stockings
non-slip socks for traction
the gown slips over his forearms and onto my shoulders
who thought to call it a gown and why are snuggies not gowns
and what are capes
these are the wrong questions

next up
a row of vinyl recliners in stark white sheets
the surgeon enters, blissful as the ponytailed nurse

everyone here is on drugs, i think. really great drugs
i don't care. i lower my gown. i'm breathing. i'm not on the verge
i couldn't care less. i lower my gown; i look at my breasts, familiar aliens
doctor crane makes a patchwork of black lines
gossips with mom about the kardashians
marks dash across my chest, a trail of ants
something about pregnant kim's waterlogged ankles; assholes
(caitlyn doesn't exist yet, which is weird)
i'm breathing. i'm fine. he smiles benevolently and vanishes
serene nurse brings me an ugly needle
his thick veins swell with ice

mr. barnes the anesthesiologist
hoists the bag i'm attached to into the air
i trail behind, anxious dog
mom hugs me before i pass through
and i am already vanishing

he gestures to the paper table
a toddler on dad's shoulder with swollen tonsils
drinking the little cup of white liquid and gently fading into his t-shirt
cradled in his thick arms until i blink elsewhere

sit, spin, sink
the room electric; mr. barnes' coiled beard full of promise
dad had a beard when he was a buffalo and when he shaved it off
the skin was loose and pale, fleshy
a clear plastic mask rests against my stubbled cheeks and the
bridge of my nose and my chin and i am breathing
"i'm doing it," i'm breathing because i'm fine
not on the verge, i'm breathing, and then
with a breath--

ORIENTATION

welcome to the first meeting of Dead Dad Club
if you'll look beneath your seat you'll find the orientation booklet
please turn to page one sorry page three
why did we include page one and two
they're just pictures of empty recliners
Jeff please take note for the next run
remove page one and two
they're not helping
page three:
welcome
we're all here for the same reason more or less
a father vanished, got hit by a bus or
jumped off a bridge in his underwear
on your birthday or on christmas morning
had a heart attack or seven got in a drunk fight
with a brick wall had his body eaten by bears
or cancer or whiskey or meth or in my father's case
a swollen bladder and a marble floor
whatever this isn't about me it's about you
and your process so congratulations
on taking the first step, now
repeat after me:
my dad is dead
my dad is dead
our dads are dead
our dads are dead
all dads are dead
all dads are dead
feels better doesn't it
no such thing as a living father
no such thing as a patriarch
fantasy, sure, but at least you're not alone
makes it easier to forget
the small days between the big days.

I'd like to take a moment
to thank our sponsors:
the Better Off Dadless Coalition
the Living Mothers Association
and the Our Dads Are Still Alive And We Have A Pretty Good Relationship But Appreciate The Work You're Doing For Children Of Dead Dads Regardless Alliance
I'd say we wouldn't be here without you
but we would—we always find each other somehow
succeeding for the benefit of ghosts
trying to fail without an echoing shame
first to empty the dishwasher
filling in the sudden chore gap
first in line for the star wars release
when it was never really Your Thing—still,
thanks to our allies for the funding
without which we wouldn't have
the catered lunch.

THE SON SWALLOWS THE KEY

when the father fades
boys creep over the hills like rogue stars hot and orange and
into the lap of the son
to feed / to get fed

after the war the father's father crawls home with
lead in his leg he sits on the couch and
withers when he can keep his fists soft and when he can't—

the father's brother starts a band and a bakery and it doesn't matter
(the son remembers that he is never the first or last—
swap out a band for an alternative lifestyle, the bakery
for a handful of half-baked hustles—and it still doesn't matter)

the father's mother dies because she is sick
and because there is no reason not to
the father's father is a short man and a television fused at the face
a cactus in a la-z-boy and the carpet is brown
but maybe it didn't used to be

the girls at mcdonald's know him by name
everybody loves him
everybody

the son's father puts a tv in the kitchen and fills the night
with the sounds of pro-wrestlers hugging
and any old sci-fi movie or turner classic something
clangs the dishes against each other like a porcelain bell choir
there is no sound like the sound of a quiet lung
or a set of yellow crooked teeth propped open forever
no sound like the soundlessness of a father's kitchen

when the memory starts to fizzle like an impending collapse
or a neuron about to fire or a pathway lined

with brown paper luminaries or the unhinging
of place and home or the collapse of the son,
and the father and his father mother brother soldier
infant emotional wet nurse wife
and the brown brown carpet and the white white sky
a plume of want and need and sacrifice and rain
on the verge of tipping across the lip of sky
and bursting the surface tension

picture the son in iowa or
whatever palm tree infested california skyline
boys scaling hills and drinking up daylight like nectar
boys like long-tongued birds without throats
emptying their ghost bellies onto everyone
boys like a rogue meteor shower
a collapsing sky
a wound after a war that ate the legs of boys everywhere
a war that opens its mouth
and swallows

ENGINE PARTS

you will live a long and ugly life—but god forbid you don't, i mean you will, but were you to not, were you to suddenly pause, i mean—your body: someone would have to do something with it.

your body is an organ, like the piano, no, a big sack of organs, not like the piano, wrapped in calcium and coated in hair. the body can be recycled, and were you to pause, not that you will but someone has to tell you, you have options.

i don't know what happens in the morning but if it were to be midnight when you paused and you had that little pink sticker on your license, someone could page a woman and she would leave her bed and smooth out her bangs, hair the color and vibrancy of cracked mud. she would bring a clipboard to your bedside. she would list out the cogs and springs and, one by one, someone would sign away each eye, your lungs if you don't smoke much, your heart if it still beats, each kidney and knee, the liver, the skin, the ligament, the marrow.

it's upsetting to do something with a body, because even when it all gets recycled, there's still so much person left in it. the clipboard can't ask everything, like, who will get your curiosity, hunger, insomnia? who will wear the weight of you, the parts inside the inside parts, the aching, the silence? who will inherit everything and what will be rejected?

were you to pause, long enough to still the whirring in your head or the thumping in your motor, would the organs even matter? or would you slip out like a single drop of oil, willing the dirt to drink?

HYSTERICAL

my mom asked if i knew about okcupid at the exact moment i was logging in
to see if i'd scared off my last date with dead dad small talk; how funny that
mom started cruising just five weeks after something in his skull just collapsed
or imploded; just hysterical that he died on a marble floor surrounded by four
pairs of unworn orthopedic shoes from the outlet mall between home and
vegas; hysterical that a shittier room would've had softer floors and maybe
hysterical the way the hotel pampered us as if to apologize, the way they escorted
us to a clone of his room and let us eat the entire mini bar even though dad said
not to touch the tiny bottles.

how could i not laugh, across from mom at the linened table room service had
delivered, when a pair of sandwiches, glass coke bottles, and a fruit platter totaled
eighty dollars. or when hours later i wandered down to dad's room and the blood
was gone but someone had left the television on as though he'd only stepped out
for ice, which meant someone scrubbed that marble floor with cnn blaring in the
background. and when i opened his suitcase how could i not laugh at the gallon
sized ziploc stuffed with stolen hotel soaps because my father––

yes, there we were, living like the kind of people that stay in computer-automated
hotel rooms with $700 minibar bills, the kind of people that eat endless
lobster in buffets, the kind of people who don't go home without insurance or
why wouldn't i laugh? how couldn't i laugh? that night, my sister let go of my
father's limp, tubed, taped hand to climb into the massive hotel bed with my
mom, and i hopped onto the rollaway to watch the lightning storm sprawling over
the desert, each hotel a tangle of christmas lights winking and shifting beneath
wild herds of electricity.

SYLLOGISM

i read an article about a dickless veteran
it said the transplant was successful, the old genitals
clinging stoically to the new host
the familiar swaying paused, a gasp between lives
a success but the psychological effects—
the story called it a failed miracle
accepted by the body but the person inside of it
the person beside of it
latched stoically to the memory of a form dead
save the memory, the prayer, the disappointment, the rebirth
the hubris

i was an article once

beneath the lights
a grooming of organs, the body cut away from itself
the body and the person inside of it pile at the foot
scalpel passing through soft butter

the transition from father to donor from organ
to transplant from his cornea to a cornea or a lung or
a liver or
a tendon
the story remains

the fall, the ectoectomy, the blank middle, the clear end:
we buried the ashes of a secondhand puzzle
the dust of a man in a box
in the soil, there was a moment
after the harvest and before the lights clicked off
when the flicker was a puppet or the shadow of a flame

coolers full, brimming with potential
the body in stitches, a crumpled paper sack piled high with clippings

and behind it the lawn is crisp, empty as a suburb
save the cooler, save the host

CONTAGION

i don't remember the first time i cried on the train but i do remember a few hours ago, surface tension straining and leaning until everything toppled out like crumbling brick. i press my face against the glass as the vents whisper into my eye sockets; i want them to dry out like fruit leather or a dirty washcloth, starched into shape.

at my deli job i fed onions into the meat slicer one by one, thin loops of purple and white shooting into a plastic tub as the machine spun and squealed inches from my fingers, my vision blurring as the shop filled with aggressive fumes. i burned as the onions sputtered and spewed but the best part was the ugly moneyed customers, suddenly sniffling without knowing why—i was contagious. i've always admired typhoid mary, who shared her germs so selflessly, unwashed fingers caressing baskets of fruit and golden loaves of bread. she fed them clams and typhoid, and when they tried to confiscate her sickness, ran, cradling her gallbladder like a secret.

i guess public transit is an island, yes, i guess this sunken tunnel is an island is atlantis is a colony for the overflowing and the broken and the breaking. i guess a train is too liminal to hurt, suspended between the insomniac city and its drowsy worms, the waking stars and their poisoned earth. where does my sickness ruminate, churning in my gut or skull like cream? i wonder if i'd cut it out of me as a tumor, or if i'd escape, disease cupped in my filthy hand until they caught me, whisked off to island full of people like this, all this rotting wood, all this toppling brick.

INTERLUDE

return to the world a newborn kitten, eyeless dough
chest sealed with glue and thread, needs time to cure
slump against the wooden chair and cradle my chest
feel the life of it straining for air
thundershirt, bundle of gauze and foam
unbutton the neck of my oversized shirt and peek
pull away the layers of fluff to find a gaping blank
slide two fingers into the void to find what's left
and there is just skin, miraculous skin
inhale and feel fragile, withdraw and button

275 days ago he collapses alone in a vegas hotel room
274 days and 18 hours ago, i board a plane at oakland international
heart galloping beneath atrophy, i do not cry on the plane
or at mccarren international, or while my mom and sister soak shoulders
or at airport slot machines, or at sbarro's, or in the black town car
dry, we wonder what would happen if he died
what a bastard he was, what if mom remarried a woman (ellen or oprah)

miles of abandoned fluorescent hallways until the icu
my cousin, an alcoholic sommelier living off the strip
meets us at the nurses' station
we see the lump of blanketed feet from the lobby, perfectly still
i want to get back in the elevator, crawl back into the town car
drive back to the airport, board the next plane back to california
bart back to my best friend's house, crawl back into her bed
go back. unbutton

a season for organ harvesting
we are told that if he doesn't die on the operating table
they will stop his heart after they retrieve the usable parts
august 17, 2012, in the early hours, a surgeon stops my father

the facts of this are simple

a man lived for 63 years, died in a hotel room
was maintained on a respirator, died again
was autopsied, cremated, placed into a plastic bag
slid into a plastic box, which my sister flew back to vegas to retrieve
then back on a plane with my father's ashes
i divided the dust for scattering and burial
never saw the body. never saw the blood

the thing about denial is it's yours

YOU SANK INTO LEE'S COUCH AND WANTED TO UNDO TIME

anyone who claims not to be codependent is a liar, and your father is no exception. he needed your need, but you don't need him anymore. mom can fix the modem herself and she has okcupid, plentyoffish, and j-date. a comedian named dale comes over to the house and kisses her on the mouth in front of you, even though he said he's not attracted to her. he hugs her too long and makes fun of deaf people and asian drivers and hugs every woman in the room. dale comes over to the house and eats mom's diet cooking because at 45 he can still barely feed himself. mom says he has a "good heart," an "equal opportunity offender."

you are learning to hold mom so she doesn't need to be held; in some oedipal twist of fate you have usurped the crown, you drive dad's car, you fixed the laptop, you transferred the ashes into jewelry bags to distribute or bury. you couldn't wash your hands afterward, and instead, massaged the dust into your skin with the thick herbal lotion mom keeps next to the sink.

of course you miss him, but maybe "miss" doesn't accurately describe it. "missing" sounds like longing. you don't miss him exactly. but he is missing in the sense that he can't be found and in the sense that he has both missed everything and is missing from everything. he missed your surgery, the entirety of grad school, the time you taught yourself to splice stereo wires and change headlights. he is missing every time the garage door opens to reveal anything that is not a cranky old man. he is missing when you park his car facing the house, instead of backed-in. he is missing when you stand in the silence of his dusty office, promising to become him. you were all forced to become new people in his absence; you wonder if he would still like you.

at the funeral, mom's friend michelle approached you to say she finally understood why you're a transsexual—someone had to be the man of the house. which is bullshit of course because you and mom and your sister are all shuffling around in his orthopedic sneakers. he had big feet with toenails shaped just like yours. you remember his feet propped up beneath the blanket, the way the doctor pressed her thumb into the nail bed of his big toe, pushing and pushing to see if his brain still knew pain and you waited and bargained. but something between the mind and toe failed to spark and his eyelids were so perfectly still and there was nothing at all. the doctor was sorry, so sorry, everyone was sorry but no one was sorrier than you, sorry for the useless knot of yourself that went tight at the airport and never quite loosened. in this way, you are missing too and you want nothing more than to be missed the way you're supposed to miss your father.

a year is just osmosis, you think. nothing more than a few layers of skin.

UNDERSTUDY

i hate everyone with a father
even the mean ones, which isn't fair
like a drunk is somehow better than
a king is somehow better than
a corpse is somehow better than an earthquake

when we were kids he wouldn't let us eat sugar, like an asshole
and gave out raisins at halloween, like an asshole
sometimes my dad worked putting a million stickers
on a million boxes on a million shelves, sometimes
we trapped leprechauns in strawberry baskets with dangling coins and
sometimes we lost the science fair or made rice-a-roni
canned corn and frozen steak for dinner
mom worked nights and dad did our laundry
washed dishes while watching oily wrestlers on the little tv

i left my shoes in the living room and
i left my clothes in the dryer and
we interrupted him and
for years his thunder mouth shook and
the earth rumbled until somebody, anybody cried and
at 15 i got high and fucked for the first time at a friend's house and
the earth rattled, cracked open, and he didn't even notice; and
his mother died of cancer before i could breathe but
i smoked in the park anyway and he didn't even notice and
i never told him anything my mom could mention for me and
he never said a word when that boy touched me

but when she told him
he looked like he was drowning, like
the house had sprung a leak and
the white carpet was wet and swollen and splitting and
when he was a boy they called him a bear or a buffalo
he used to steel himself for our tiny fists and laugh

as we hammered uselessly at the wall behind his belly
when she told him, they gave me a feather pillow and said
show us what you want to do to that boy
and i did
his gut must have leapt watching
the muscles unafraid, tense as the wave before the crash
frozen, with no fight but a fighting stillness
a silence for a fresh wound, a quiet as thick as ointment
clean as air

if he had known
if i had known, if i could have abandoned the sticky recollection
stirred it into the ashes we trapped below stone
if the stubbornness, the persistence of it all
could have been shoveled into the incinerator beside him
would it have even fit?

HERE ARE SOME TIPS FOR GROCERY SHOPPING

you will need coupons, hundreds of them. i suggest a blue nylon pouch with fraying edges and a silver snap to hold everything in place. if you're organized you'll use your coupons before they expire and if you're not you'll just have to clean the envelope out every weekend while clipping the new ones. don't be fooled into thinking a newspaper is anything but kindling covered coupons and a sheet of lukewarm comic strips with which to torture your children.

(for the record, you know pearls before swine loses its comedic impact when it has to pass through your mouth before your kids can hear it. it drives them crazy but announcing the punch lines serves the dual purpose of irritating them and letting you feel like a penguin vomiting into the mouths of its young. you, the provider, the nurturer, squeezing through front door flanked by bags the size of full garbage liners stuffed with coats that might fit. you the hunter-gatherer, making endless trips between the house and a minivan trunk packed with double bagged groceries. love wrapped in plastic, better than pureed fish wrapped in stomach acid.)

which brings me back to groceries. effective shopping requires strategy; lists, tactical maneuvers. imagine your family as a squadron of fighter jets, less flashy than the blue angels but every bit as patriotic. divide and conquer. send the oldest girl to find things she can't fuck up, shelf stable condiments or discontinued novelty ice cream, teach the younger girl to look at the impulse candies by the register with her eyes and not with her hands. teach them both to dangle from the nose of your cart, counterweighted by fragrant cantaloupes and packages of store brand pasta and graying meats on "manager's special" to stash in the garage freezer.

carry a calculator, in case cell phones haven't been invented yet. divide the cost of the cottage cheese by the weight; find the price per ounce. do this for every brand and size container of cottage cheese. find the cheapest per ounce. put it in the cart amidst protests from little girls who only like the knudsen brand on their pasta. when you get home, realize they're right, and that knudsen is far superior to kraft or any store brand, the alternates too tart or dry or soupy, and knudsen, perfectly smooth beneath its lid until stirred into a creamy, tender sea of curds to be spooned over hot margarined pasta cooked several minutes too long, a hot-cold flurry of lactose and starch. the girls like everything you cook: the half moons of brick red kosher salami fried in margarine and drenched in scrambled egg, the american cheese sandwiches on white bread with margarine. the rice-a-roni, the hamburger helper, the delicate golden slices of toasted challah from the only bakery in town that makes it. all of it glistening beneath a perfect sheen of country crock.

when the candy bars inevitably go on sale, slip one into each girl's palm, watch their eyes bulge at the unbelievable heft of an entire milky way in a tiny clenched fist. the older girl likes the dark chocolate ones, the younger, milk. stash this away next to the note about knudsen's, the place that could eventually catalogue the older one's inevitable teenage vegetarianism, the list of gelatin-free gummy candies to stock the glove box with, or the brand of tampons your wife prefers and the best deal on canned fruit or cake mix. do not forget to buy peanut m&m's. you will want them when you settle into your makeshift garage office to watch action films or professional wrestling, to masturbate and fall asleep sitting up with your hand still perched on the mouse, jaw slack and eyelids fluttering in the stale air.

in the morning, the girls will jump into your bed and wiggle into the blanket valley between you and your wife. you will think about the cubes of cut cantaloupe in the fridge, how much longer until they rot, how to convince the girls to snack on fruit when there's cheese to be had. they want breakfast. while they eat, noisily, you will sit at the table and pore over newspaper inserts for deals on paper towels, paper napkins, and paper plates. diet soda. fat-free ranch dressing. cans of tomato sauce. processed cheese. frozen vegetables. look for the manufacturer's coupons and cross-reference the store sales to maximize your discounts. don't be afraid to shop at multiple stores. don't be afraid to take hours. when you get home, dissect the ribbons of receipt paper with a highlighter. what did you spend? what did you save? tell anyone. tell everyone.

here are some tips for grocery shopping: smile your crooked smile when the clerk recognizes you and calls you mr. coupon because here, of all places, you are titled. in the grocery store aisles, you're a strategist, a mathematician, and a gambler. in the checkout line, you're shameless about the stack of clippings you trade for food.

you disowned the shame ages ago, left it for the perturbed cashier waiting to go on lunch, or for your daughters to shovel into their backpacks, to keep and to save, to bag and to carry.

TWELVE STEPS FOR DATING YOUR FATHER

1. you are your own footprint. you have become unmanageable. you have two identical feet and one is sinking into the earth.

2. there is a god. he doesn't like caramel, fresh vegetables, or paying full price.

3. do not interrupt him. do not argue and do not cry except for when he wants you to. do not become his father. do not leave your shoes on the floor and be sure to make your bed, make your lunch, eat his cooking. try to understand. turn yourself over like a dusty stone, startle what lies beneath.

4. do not mention his teeth. instead, check your own. inventory the molars, incisors, bicuspids. the canines. he is afraid of dogs.

5. god's son doesn't like chocolate, avocados, cheese, or anything with a sauce. he prefers salted caramel cupcakes and shoving them into your mouth mid-orgasm, wrestling in the kitchen and fucking on the bus, sleeping in your armpit, and bathing in a river.

6. if you want to heal, do not speak to the son in the morning or before reiki, do not step on his yoga mat, do not talk about yourself until you ask about him, do not expect him to use protection, do not ask when he is coming home, do not ask when he is leaving, do not ask if he's done yet, do not ask him how he's doing—ask him how his body is instead, ask him if he wants something but also if he needs something. there will always be two answers. neither will save you.

7. do not mention his teeth. do not interrupt him. do not tell him how much he resembles his father. or your father. or any father. offer him your hand, or foot.

8. he met your mother in a 12-step program. do not ask which one.

9. to apologize, god will teach you how to hide your candy, take apart anything and maybe put it back together, how to sleep with your mouth open and your eyes rolled back, how to turn things off and on and off again, how to yell at your mother, how to sauté mushrooms, how to drive yourself to school, how to care for someone else's parents, how to have a father and how to hate him softly, how to work forever, how to laugh loud enough to garner stares, how to pour butter and salt over fat-free popcorn, how to cry at a musical, how to yell until your eyes bulge. he will apologize before there is a reason to.

10. it was overeaters anonymous.

11. clasp your hands together. don't touch the radio, the air conditioning, the dishwasher, or anything else with a dial. there is a frequency just beyond your reach.

12. when they leave, when you leave, don't conflate the hollows in their mouths. keep their photographs tucked between your perfect molars, the echo of their hands on your shoulder blades, their handwriting filed under your own name. keep your footing. mind the gap.

EPILOGUE

the balboa island ferry
teeters under the weight of us
mom rolls down windows, stuffs the minivan with salt
a seal slips through pitching water
 hungry seagulls, screaming pelicans
zitty sun-bleached teenagers meander down narrow aisles
collecting wrinkled fares from passengers and cars
spitting out change from the metal coin belt
my mouth is coated in sticky pink candy
from a woman demanding bible verses as payment
i didn't know any, tried a commandment instead
honor thy taffy

driving on water consumes me for years
a car wash on the way to saturday breakfast
dad wheeling into the dark tunnel
the clicking and whirring of its machinery
the furious downpour of white soap
the thunderstorm that fills us with lightning
swirling brushes that flap against the car doors
threatening to bust through
water rips the foam off in sheets
a slow roll through the blow drier
droplets creeping up the windshield in reverse
sprung into hyperdrive

the tunnel ejects us damp and glittering
 dry summer heat
dad jumps out with a fistful of pilfered napkins
wiping down the side mirrors and hubcaps
before the water spots set
afterward
he takes us to mcdonald's
splits a value breakfast between the three of us

extra hash browns for the kids

at 25 i spent my summer attempting to reassemble
handed six dollars to an apathetic gas station attendant
eased dad's car into a tunnel
heaved over the hump
rolled until red 'x' became a green check
ten filthy months since i inherited the car
almost a year in my unwashed care
the mechanisms jolted to life
robotic mops and pumps firing at the windows
clawing at the bird shit and bug corpses
i turned up the radio to mask my glee
clapping like a happy baby, swallowed by sudsy walls
laughing or choking, whatever
how good it felt to vanish
afterward
i needed a root beer float
eyed the mcbreakfast menu, tongued the memory
ordered the largest fries you can legally sell
drove home, sucking on greasy fingers
the wheel spinning in my spare hand

i've never ridden the ferry here
and wonder how it would feel to putter across the bay
on a gas-powered raft speckled with humans
fog weaving into gravity-defiant ponytails
i think coit tower would make a decent substitute
for the balboa island ferris wheel
spokes jutting sleepily into the low gray mist
promising to remember

ACKNOWLEDGEMENTS

I would like to thank the Bay Area Trans Writers Workshop, and in particular, Zach Ozma, for their tireless editing over the life of this chapbook. Additionally, I'm indebted to my mother, Gail, and my sister, Laura, for their unwavering support and their collectively twisted sense of humor. Lastly, a shout-out to my dad, who always encouraged me to translate my life experiences into poetry, in spite of mixed results throughout high school. Thanks, all.

JULIAN SHENDELMAN has a weird-looking dog (part fawn, part fruit bat) and a nice Jewish boyfriend. A ten-year resident of Oakland, Julian splits his time between his boring desk job, organizing the Bay Area Trans Writers Workshop, and making moody zines. Julian identifies as "genre-fluid." He was a 2016 Pushcart-nominated poet for his piece in *Bat City Review*, and won a literary death match with a true story about Queer Punk Cannibalism. This is his first book.